Roy/Shevlin Chronicles

∽

by
Jeanne Shevlin Gates

Roy/Shevlin Chronicles
Copyright © 2018
Jeanne Shevlin Gates

All rights reserved.
This publication may not be reproduced, stored in a retrieval system, or transmitted in any form: recording, mechanical, electronic, or photocopy, without written permission of the publisher.
The only exception is brief quotations used in book reviews.

ISBN 978-1-941069-83-7

Prose Press Pawleys Island SC 29585
prosencons@live.com

DEDICATION

*This memoir is dedicated to my parents,
Emmett and Phyllis Roy Shevlin.
They established moral and ethical values
that have been the foundation of
all their descendants.*

Wedding Picture

life in motion
ever changing gift
moving forward
a force beyond our control

ACKNOWLEDGEMENT

Thank you to my family for all my great memories. If I was able to turn back time and pick a family, I wouldn't change a thing.

If it wasn't for my friends and mentors, this journey would not have been taken and the memories of all those special relatives would be forgotten, lost in time.

Darlene Eichler, a warm and inspiring teacher and also an accomplished author, guided me in writing my memories and encouraged me along the way.

To my friends, Kathy, Dee and Kay, and members of my writing classes, thank you for being patient, and helping me find my voice.

Phyllis O'Brien Stinehour has spent many hours collecting pictures and information and has made our family memoir possible.

TABLE OF CONTENTS

Dedication

Acknowledgement

Introduction 1

The Family Of George Roy 3

Learning Bar Room Songs
   And Other Fun Stories 7

The Siblings Of George Roy 11

Maude Edith Roy 13

Aunt Maudie's Family Secret 14

George And Delia Landry Roy 16

George Roy 17

The Family Of Delia Landry Roy 19

Delia Josephine Landry Roy 22

Whitefield, New Hampshire 23

Home Remedies 25

Children Of George And Delia Roy. 29

Aunt Amelia's Bloomers 31

TABLE OF CONTENTS

Gertrude Maria Roy Williams 36
Eva Roy 39
Cleo Thomas Benton Roy 44
My Barnyard Playmates 45
Berlin, New Hampshire 54
Enduring Parochial School 57
The Family Of Emmett Patrick Shevlin 64
The Children Of Patrick And Mary Shevlin 66
Phyllis Eirleen Roy Shevlin 74
Emmett Patrick Shevlin 77
Jeanne Patricia Ann Shevlin Gates 79
Skating Days 83
Ralph Emmett Patrick Shevlin 91
Family Reunion Pictures 94
Our Family Geneology 97

INTRODUCTION

At the funeral of my ninety-six year old Aunt Tootsie, my cousin Phyllis Stinehour turned to me and said, "Jeannie, do you realize that we are now the two oldest women in the family?"

"No way!" I just couldn't believe that time had slipped by so quickly. Where had all those years gone?

The memoir idea began to incubate, and now in the midst of writing our family chronicles, I realize that many of our family members are gone. All those pictures that we have in boxes, albums, and on the wall will have to be collected and hopefully identified. The process of compiling all this information has been a sentimental journey.

If you are reading this, you are probably a family member, relative or a friend. My goal is to introduce you to those members of our family that you never got to meet and to tell you all the tall tales that were retold many times at family reunions or on long winter nights in the kitchen.

Growing up on a farm in New Hampshire in the 1940s was a special time, not only because it was a wonderful place to live but we experienced a memorable time in history.

I assure you that these stories are from my memory alone, and others may recall events differently. If you are frantically looking ahead to see if your name is mentioned in family events or exposed in secrets, you'll just have to read on.

THE FAMILY OF GEORGE ROY

Louis Roy was George Roy's great grandfather and married Perpetua ____. They were married in Magog, Quebec in the 1800s. They had one son, Alexander, born in 1855. Perpetua had one son from a previous marriage, Pierre Henri.

Alexander Roy, George's grandfather, was born in Lennonville, Quebec in 1855. He married Celina Toussaint from Warwick, Quebec and they moved to Island Pond, Vt. in 1911. In the spring of 1912, they moved to Whitefield, N.H.

Alexander was employed at the engine house in Whitefield. He and Celina had thirteen children. Olive (1880), Lilly (1883), Laura (1883), Dolor (1889), Henry (1890) , were lost in infancy. Surviving children were George, Bertha, Eva, Maude, Henry, Alice, Emile, and Alfred.

Celina's parents were Aimey Toussaint and Domitile Gamelin. Domitile remarried and had four children, Emme (1897), Helen Hildreth (1901), Nellie Hildreth (1861), Edward Hildreth (1862).

Alexander Roy – George Roy's father

Celina Toussaint Roy – wife of Alexander Roy

Henry Roy – George's brother

Phyllis Roy, Waldo Roy, and Geraldine Roy in the "roadster"

Alice Roy Berard, unknown female, Maude Roy Savoie

Maude Roy Savoie and Phyllis Roy

Emile (Pete) Roy, wife Bernadette, Delia Landry Roy

Emile and Bernadette

Emile as an altar boy

Maude Roy

Bernice Berard Nigro
(Alice'sdaughter)

LEARNING BAR ROOM SONGS AND OTHER FUN STORIES

I sure wish that every kid could have grown up on a farm in rural America back in the 1940's. My grandfather's farm was in Whitefield, New Hampshire. I lived there with my mother and her family when my father was serving in the Army in Korea. While the world was tearing itself apart, our little corner of the world was insulated. I'd like to tell you about our farm, my relatives, and I hope to give you a glimpse into the life we led back then.

My grandfather, George Roy, also known as Pa or Jay, settled in Whitefield in 1906, and bought a piece of land on Water Street Extension. It was a pretty big piece of property, big enough to sell off some of it to a sawmill company, where he and his horse, Junie, worked for many years. It was most likely the source of the lumber he used for the house. He built his house in 1906, and it still stands today, looking solid, testament to his building skills. The house had a large front porch and an attached barn. It's a good thing he thought of a porch, because it sure got a lot of use over the years, being a place where everyone rocked and talked.

When I recall that barn of my youth, it is very large in my mind. I never got used to that blast of urine and manure smell when I first opened the large wooden door with leather hinges. It had a large section for hay and rafters up high for scary jumping, and the rest was stalls for the animals. Junie, of course, had the biggest stall, another for the cow who had no name, and an empty stall which belonged to Dick, another work horse that probably died from old age and hard work.

Between the barn and the house was a large room used for storage and grain barrels (where Pa hid his Ballantine Ale bottles). It was also where my grandmother would sit on a stool, churning butter from the cream on top of the milk from our large metal milk cans. That took way too long for me to stand around and watch.

In those days, the kitchen was the biggest room in the house. Against one wall was our expandable maple table. That table saw lots of meals, heard lots of conversations and was used almost nightly for family gatherings for Canasta, Flinch or Steal the Old Lady's Bundle (my favorite). My Aunt Tootsie kept that table in her apartment until she was ninety-six years old. The big maple chair seats were worn silky smooth by then. The wooden bowl with wax fruit also survived a century. During that time, the fruit was deformed by scars from many sets of teeth of generations of Roy and Shevlin children who thought that fruit was really real.

The wood stove was huge, taking up one whole corner of the kitchen, and I can still smell the wood that we burned for heat and cooking. Next to the stove was a basket of wood shavings and logs, and on the wall a metal holder for sulfa tipped matches. Pa left his frying pan on the back of the stove with fatback grease in it and nobody dared wash it.

Tootsie was a twin to Eva who died shortly after birth. They were very tiny, born at home as were most babies. There was no hospital with incubators to keep them warm so they were both placed on a large pillow on the open oven door.

The outside of our house was the fun part. I rarely like to stay inside. There was a big pig sty that smelled really bad, and the baby pigs were so cute, especially when they all lined up to nurse with their curly tails showing. The pigs ate our leftovers, called slop, which we emptied into their trough. Really awful smelly stuff but they made a lot of noise eating it up.

Then, there was the henhouse. Pa had a sense of humor that wasn't always funny to me. He would send me into the henhouse to collect eggs. The first time he didn't tell me to watch out for the rooster. Holding my big egg basket on my arm, I slowly opened the door. The rooster was waiting and attacked me. I screamed and ran out of the henhouse. I didn't think that was funny at all but Pa sure did. The next time I went in, I waited until I saw that rooster out in the yard, and snuck in to collect the eggs. Pa would always put some glass eggs in the nests. I guess that was to trick the hens into thinking that they were doing a good job. Sometimes the hens would lay eggs under the barn and since I was the only small person that could reach the eggs, under the barn I would crawl. My mother and Ma (I'll tell you about them soon), must have been mad when Pa sent me under the barn because it was near the manure pile and I would need a bath and fresh clothes afterwards.

I'll tell you more about Pa. He taught me that my name was Jeannie Bullshit. Every time I answered to this name, everyone laughed, so I loved to repeat it over and over and over. That is, until Father Carrigan came down to the farm one Sunday morning to give Ma communion because she was too sick to go to Mass. When he came in and saw me, he bent over and said, "What a cute little girl. What's your name?"

Of course, smiling, I replied, "Jeannie Bull…, at which point my mother put her hand over my mouth and said, "She doesn't speak very plainly."

Pa would sit me on his lap and teach me lots of barroom songs, which I memorized with amazing speed. I'M ONLY A BIRD IN A GILDED CAGE was our favorite duet and there were many other songs in which I was fluent, but they don't bear repeating. One of his favorite games was "count our toes." He would have me count my toes, and then count his. I always got twelve when I counted his and only ten when I counted mine. Yes, he had twelve toes.

Now, about my grandmother, who was affectionately known as Ma or Little Mammy. She was always busy sewing, cooking, or washing clothes in a big tub and rubbing them on a metal board. She would pin the clothes on long clotheslines out back and on windy days you could see the sheets flapping away. Boy, could she cook. She made bread every day, and we always had pies or cakes for dessert. Every meal we had potatoes and we used pork fat for margarine. There were no supermarkets then, so we ate chicken, beef or pork, either from our own animals or bought from neighbors. (Maybe that's why the cow had no name because often there was a different cow in the barn.)

Ma was also a great seamstress and she made all my dresses from the grain sack material. Some had lots of ruffles. Those were special dresses that I wore to Sunday Mass. She and Pa were up early every day when it was still dark. I don't recall seeing her relaxing much, except on the front porch at night. After supper, everyone sat on the porch or in the kitchen, talking or playing cards. There were no televisions yet, but we had a radio that we listened to for news and music. Sometimes my Uncle Cleo would come down with his family and he would play the guitar and sing or play the spoons. To play the spoons you took two large spoons, belly to belly and hit them against your leg, making sounds like a drum. He was a really good singer and he liked Western music.

You're probably wondering about my mother. Her name was Phyllis and she was the youngest of all the Roy children. She worked as a telephone operator when we lived at the farm and also helped at home with cooking and cleaning. Well, not so much with the cooking. She would kill me for telling you this, but she was not the best cook in the family. Maybe because she was the baby and everyone else cooked. Even though she may not have been a good cook, she was the smartest, I think.

Stay tuned for some funny stories about our life and what we did for fun.

THE SIBLINGS OF GEORGE ROY

EMILE EDWARD (PETE) ROY 10/9/1897 – 10/1/1964
Pete and George were very close and raised their families in Whitefield. Pete married Helen Hildreth and they had two children, Waldo and Geraldine.
> Waldo and his wife, Dorothy, had two children,
>> Robert and Dorothy.
> Geraldine married Nathan McClure and had five children,
>> Mary Ann, Patty Jean, Dennis, Nathan Jr., and Carol.

Mary Ann and Patty were my childhood friends and I often spent time with them when I was in Whitefield.

BERTHA ROY 1888
Bertha married George John and had three children,
> Estelle, Leo and Verla.

EVA ROY 1883
Eva died at the age of 16

HENRY ROY 1890
Henry married Charlotte Perkins (his second wife), and had two children.

ALFRED JOSEPH ARTHUR ROY 1894
Fred married Hazel Henry and had one daughter,
> Ruth. Ruth married George Blight and had two children,
>> Marilyn May and Judith Arlene.

ALICE ROY 1/13/71

Alice married John Hubert (Frenchy) Berard. They had three children,

Bernice, Anita and Roy.

Bernice married Dominic Nigro and had three children, Joseph, Jane and Michael. I recall Bernice fondly and remember her great smile and genuine friendliness.

Roy married Dot Haynes and had five children,

Cheryl, Debbie, Kevin, and twins, Jennifer and Jeffrey.

Roy remained in the Whitefield area and raised his family in a beautiful farmhouse near the Waumbek Hotel.

MAUDE EDITH ROY
9/9/1892 – 11/11/1963

Aunt Maudie was one of the most interesting members of our family and I wish everyone could have met her. She was large in every way :her body, her smile, the way she cooked from her Fanny Farmer cookbooks, how she could out talk anybody and did, married twice at a time that it was scandalous and was the subject of our only family mystery.

She was George's older sister and her home was just around the corner from George's farm. She married Thomas Hartwell and the marriage lasted over twenty years. Thomas was an accomplished stone mason and the decorative stone wall he built at the Mountain View Hotel still stands. After his death, Maudie married Joseph Savoie, who was previously married to Thomas Hartwell's mother. Bet that was the scandal of the day back then!

Maudie always reminded me of Mrs. Santa Claus. She wore small round rimless glasses, always had a smile, gave big hugs and loved to cook for everyone. I can still smell the beans and molasses she had simmering on the back of her wood stove.

 My mother and Tootsie would send me over to Maudie's on errands and it didn't take long for me to figure out why they didn't go themselves. She LOVED to talk and when she started, I was her captive audience. I can still see her rocking back and forth in her oversized rocker, and hear the clicking of her false teeth as she spoke. I was totally mesmerized by her stories.

Being an accomplished cook, she was retained by many families near the Mountain Vies to be their cook and housekeeper. She was also employed by the Secretary of the Interior, Sinclair Weeks, at his summer home in Lancaster, N.H.

AUNT MAUDIE'S FAMILY SECRET

Well, I know you are all waiting to hear about our only family secret, at least, the only one I knew about.

Aunt Maudie always had interesting stories and I would sit for hours while she rocked in her big wicker rocker and clicked her teeth as she talked. One afternoon, she began to whisper, and put her fingers to her lips, saying, "I'm going to tell you a secret that only you and I will know. Do you promise never to tell anyone?" This was the first time anyone had ever asked me to keep a secret, so I replied, "Yes, I promise to keep our secret until I die." I figured that this whole secret thing was pretty serious and I had read about swearing to keep a secret until you die, so I figured I'd better say it too. As it turned out, it was probably the only secret that I ever kept so long.

She told me that her husband, Tommy, had built a secret room in their house, and he made moonshine there. I had heard about moonshine from eavesdropping on conversations and knew that it was something like beer that Pa drank. Maudie said it was against the law to make moonshine and although Tommy was already dead, she wanted it to remain a secret.

"Could I see the room, Aunt Maudie?"

"Well, I don't think that would be a good idea. Where the room is has to be part of the secret."

Several years later, Aunt Tootsie asked Maudie to come over and spend the night during a bad storm. Maudie brought along all her important papers, like her will. In the morning, she returned home. The next day, Tootsie was concerned because she had not seen Maudie outside her house, so she went over to check on her. She found Maudie in bed, as if asleep. She had died during the night, alone in her big house.

At this time I was in high school and attended the funeral with my family. As the family gathered after the funeral, the conversation turned to Maudie's missing will and other important papers. Maybe this was the time to tell the long kept secret. I piped up and said, "Did you look in Tommy's secret room where he made moonshine?"

There was a sudden silence and a lot of blank stares. My mother and Tootsie began to smile. My Mom said, "Who told you that?"

"Maudie told me about the secret room where Tommy made moonshine years ago and made me promise never to tell anyone. I figured that this was a good time to tell you since it's probably where she kept important papers."

Knowing looks and raised eyebrows were seen, and it looked like everyone thought I was crazy. Maybe they all thought that it was just another one of Maudie's tall tales.

Those papers were never found, and as the years passed and I traveled by her old house, I often wondered if any of the future tenants ever found a secret room.

GEORGE AND DELIA ROY

This family history begins with George and Delia Roy. They were married in Island Pond, Vt. on March 6, 1905. They had nine children, seven who survived to adulthood.

George built their home on Water Street in Whitefield, N.H. in 1906 and he and Delia raised their children there.

Jay

Jay and
Emmett Shevlin

GEORGE ROY
5/28/85 – 10/14/63

George Roy, also known as Pa or Jay, was born in Capelton Mines, Quebec in 1885. He had 7 siblings. At the age of 17, he and his brother, Emile (Pete), decided to walk to Whitefield, New Hampshire from Island Pond, Vermont to look for work, a distance of about 50 miles. For some reason, there were a lot of men in our family that were called Pete, even though this was not their given name, so you will see this name appear frequently. George and Pete settled in Whitefield, built their own homes and raised their families there.

Pa was a stern looking man, not often smiling. He was short by present day standards, but solidly built, sun had weathered his face and a life of hard work had left indelible lines. He was always seen wearing his jockey cap, and when he took it off, the white skin of his prematurely bald head was in sharp contrast to his face and neck. To say that he was a hard worker who cared for his family would be an understatement. The house he built in the early 1900's still stands today and looks pretty solid even now. The farm had one horse, Junie, one cow, lots of pigs and chickens, the cat, Simone, and the dog, Bunny.

The grain barrel in the barn was his hiding place for his Ballantine Ale bottles. As he worked to excess, he drank to excess. His drinking caused our family a lot of pain in many ways. In spite of this, there were some stories that I can recall with humor.

I can picture his white wicker rocker in the big kitchen near the window that overlooked the back fields. The brass spittoon sat on the floor to the left and his smoking stand near his right elbow. I can still smell the cherry aroma from the tobacco in his pipe. When he was drinking, he liked to sing. As a small child, sitting on his lap, he taught me lots of bawdy songs.

Pa was the picture of health, and died quietly in his sleep at the age of 78.

LUNENBURG VETERINARIAN SCHOOL
DEPARTMENT OF HORSE SENSE, SPECIALIZING IN HORSE DOCTORING [PILLS & SALVES]

BE IT KNOWN TO ALL THAT

George A. Roy
ALIAS GEORGE KING, ALIAS JAY

LONG NOTED for his Horse Sense and General Horsing around and good kind Horsemanship, and never once getting the Horselaugh, and always being a lover of strong Horse-radish is hereby presented with an

Honorary License for Horse Doctoring

SEALED, SIGNED AND PRESENTED ON MAY 28, 1955

By *A. Lotta Hogwash*

Honorary License made by Lawrence Stinehour

THE FAMILY OF DELIA LANDRY ROY

Guillaume Mathurin Landry (2/3/1623 – 1/8/1689) married
Gabrielle Barre (1628 – 7/4/1688)
Magliore Landry (?father of Joseph Landry)

Joseph Landry married Josephine Halle and had two children
    Henry Landry (7/9/1890 -) Henry Landry was a son from Joseph's second marriage. He was last seen on board a military ship in 1928
    Delia Landry (12/14/1985 – 4/9/51) married George Roy and had eight children
    Joseph (Pete) Landry (3/17/88 – 2/3/52) married Bernadette Langlais (1/26/90 – (8/30/81) and had nine children
        Pauline (9/5/26) married and had five children
        Jeannette (3/4/13) married ___Gagnon and had six children
        Jean Paul (1/15/31) married and had two children
        Therese (10/15/21) married Michael Trembley and had twochildren
        Leo (12/19/19) Married and had four children
        Simone (5/5/14) married and had five children
        Robert (3/25/16) married and had five children
        Madeline (6/5/18) married ___ - no children
        Roger (7/5/23) married and had four children

Bernadette with children
Pauline (11), Jean Paul (6)
taken in 1937

Josephine Halle mother of
Delia Landry Roy

Joseph (Pete) Alfred Landry (1950)
Delia Landry Roy's brother

Children of Joseph and Bernadette: left to right: Jean Paul,
Pauline, Roger, Therese, Leo, Robert, Jeanne
missing are Simone and Madeline

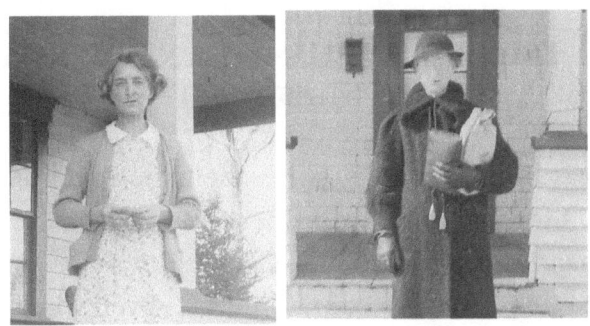

Delia Landry Roy

Delia with Carol and Pudgy Williams, Joan Roy

DELIA JOSEPHINE LANDRY ROY
12/14/1885 – 4/9/1951

Delia was born in Berlin, N.H., the eldest of three children. There is no information regarding her parents.

Delia married my grandfather, George Roy, in Island Pond, Vt. on March 6, 1905. They had nine children, seven who survived to adulthood.

Delia had a strength about her, like Pa. There was a quietness in her demeanor, going about her daily life with perseverance and strength, enduring long days and few creature comforts. Somehow, she fades from my memory, and stories that I recall are mostly ones that family members have repeated.

In person, she was tiny, frail, and I have no memory of her smiling. Her household was run like a military operation, no frills, and everyone had their chores. Her home was squeaky clean, and I think I inherited her OCD cleaning gene. Her seamstress skills were well known and her meals four star. No mixes in those days, everything made from scratch.

Discipline was strict and I found out one day just how strict she was. She found me playing with matches. My hand was turned palm up, the match lit, and blown out, and then she placed it on my palm. Needless to say, I never played with matches again.

She was ill for years with angina and died from congestive heart failure at the age of sixty-six.

Recently, information about a Landry family has surfaced and it these are our ancestors, they can be traced back to the 1600's.

WHITEFIELD, NEW HAMPSHIRE

The tiny town of Whitefield, with only 34 square miles, has an interesting history. It was the last town granted under the English provincial government and was chartered on July 4, 1774. It was incorporated in 1804. The name may have derived from a famous English evangelist, George Whitefield, or may have originated from references to snowy white fields in the surrounding mountains.

When the railroad made its way into the area, so did the tourists. Many came from the large East coast cities in the summers and a popular spot was the Mountain View Grand Resort established in 1866. This hotel has undergone extensive renovations and is still a luxurious relaxing destination today. It overlooks Mount Washington and the entire presidential range, Mount Monroe, Mount Adams, Mount Jefferson and Mount Madison.

The population of Whitefield in 2010 was 2300, but in my childhood in the early 1940's, it was probably higher.

As a child, I can recall the big central common with a bandstand, and lots of sidewalks and benches. The common area was circled by many stores, including the Rexall Drug Store, where I enjoyed many ice cream cones. In the winter, the common area was flooded and ice skating was popular. In the summer, the locals brought their chairs and enjoyed local musicians playing in the bandstand on Sunday afternoons.

One of the busiest stores was the grain store, complete with a decorative fountain where horses could get a refreshing drink of water while waiting for their owners to shop. I loved going into the grain store with Pa to see the baby chicks.

The side streets had beautiful big homes, churches, and in the distance you could see a ring of high mountains, complete with snow a good part of the year.

Today, it hasn't changed much, the common is still there, but there is an air of nostalgia for a town that has known a great history. Traffic still travels around the green, passes the mostly empty stores, but when you look in the distance, the mountains are still as beautiful.

I still love visiting the old farmstead to recall happy memories.

Whitefield Common

HOME REMEDIES

Ma was in charge of our health. She had lots of home remedies that had been passed from generation to generation. Fortunately for me, I wasn't sick very often, but when I was, she always had the perfect solution. She even had medicines to keep me well.

First, was cold prevention. She would cut up onions, sprinkle sugar on them, and cover them for the night. I can still see the white ceramic bowl with a saucer on top, on the pantry shelf. In the morning, I was given a teaspoon of the onion liquid. Actually, it tasted pretty good. The onion juice probably gave me such bad breath that I scared the germs away.

In case you don't know what a pantry is, our pantry was a long room off the kitchen. The counters were long so more than one person could be fixing something. There were bins that pulled out and they were for sacks of flour and sugar. We all spent a lot of time in the pantry preparing meals and it was fun when they put me on a chair to help. But that wasn't often.

Mrs. LeVasseur and son at store

The absolutely worst prevention medicine was Father John's Elixir. Every morning without fail, I was chased and given a teaspoon of the poison that was supposed to make me strong. It must have had cod liver oil in it, because it tasted and smelled so bad. Not being a dumb child, I soon learned that if I held it in my mouth, I could sneak into the den, and deposit it under the cushion of the Morris chair. It had a horsehair lining, and years later, you know who inherited that very chair. Thankfully, the lining had been replaced by then.

I must have had a taste problem. There were a lot of foods I didn't like. Ma insisted that liver was good for my blood so it was fried in with pork to fool me. That didn't work. They tried tricking me with veal, too. You can add veal, pork, and horseradish to the Father John's Elixir list. Pa tried tricking me by putting horseradish on my bread instead of bacon fat. He smiled when the tears ran down my face. That's why I don't like horseradish.

Aspergum was my favorite medicine for a fever…aspirin and gum…a medicine and a treat. Whenever I had an upset stomach, like the time I ate too many chocolate covered peanuts and threw up thirteen times, Ma made me wintergreen tea to settle my stomach.

Ma and the other women in the family spent lots of time making meals. We had fresh baked bread every day. I loved the smell of bread cooking and couldn't wait until it was done. Tootsie made the best rhubarb pie and Ma made the best chicken and dumplings.

One of my jobs was to go out into the vegetable garden to pick vegetables for supper. Sometimes I was delayed because I sat down to eat a carrot or tomato. If Ma decided to have chicken that night for supper, that meant Pa would have to kill a chicken. Too many times he tried to make me watch, but I kept my eyes closed. I remember the chicken running around without a head. When I had to stand on a chair over the kitchen sink, plucking out chicken feathers, I didn't like that job.

Sometimes Ma would send me next door to LeVasseur's Store to pick up something she needed at the last minute. I had to crawl through a barbed wire fence, walk across a hay field and into their driveway. It was a tiny store like a doll house. My Mom had a big scar on her leg from that fence, so I was pretty careful.

I remember when we first bought store margarine. It was in a plastic tube with a yellow ball inside. You had to keep squeezing the margarine until the ball broke and made the margarine yellow.

Most of the time, we just used the fat left over from cooking to put on bread.

I loved to listen to the radio in the den, curled up in the Morris chair. (Yes, the same one) The whole family liked it when I was quiet, which wasn't often except when I was eating. I listened to the Lone Ranger and Tonto, Amos and Andy, the Green Hornet, and sometimes Tootsie let me play her big band 78 records. The record player was under the radio and Tootsie helped me place the phonograph needle on the record so it wouldn't get scratched.

As well as being an early talker, I was an early reader. Tootsie or my mom took me often to get books at the library. I even had my own library card with my name on it. At first, I got the big books with only pictures, but pretty soon, I got books with words, too. Once I started school and learned to read better, I can recall sitting in the den at the farm reading the entire series of Cherry Ames nurse books. My favorite book was Girl of the Limberlost.

Playing outside was fun even if the weather wasn't good. In the winter, bundled in snowsuits, my cousin Joanie and I built snowmen, forts and caves in deep snow. We rode our sleds down hills or for a change, used a piece of linoleum. When we came in, frozen mittens and all, it took quite a while to peel off the icy layers. For hours you could smell the aroma of burning wool coming from the radiators or stoves where our wet clothes were placed to defrost. The first thing we did when we came in was to run to the bathroom. Getting in and out of snowsuits is too hard so we waited until the last minute.

Summers were too short so we almost never played inside when it was nice out. I rode my tricycle in the yard and up the dirt road. If Pa was home from work, he would put me on top of Junie for a ride. When it was really hot, we all went for a dip in the back pasture at Baby's Bathtub. There was a bend in the river that created a shallow swimming pool. It was a perfect place to cool off and even have a little picnic.

The Sunday papers were anticipated because they had paper dolls that I could cut out. First, I would cut out the doll and then cut out all the clothes she would wear, placing them over the doll with paper tabs to hold them in place. If they didn't get thrown away or lost, the dolls and clothes were saved in a cigar box from week to week.

The front porch had my swing and a big sofa swing hanging from the ceiling. The sofa was metal with arms and lined with a heavy blanket. For hours, I could be found on my swing, talking and singing. I knew a lot of songs, but the ones Pa taught me I had to sing quietly to myself. Sometimes my mom would come out and join me and we would swing together on the sofa. We didn't have a lot of time alone and this time was special because we could tell each other secrets.

One big secret I told her was that Tootsie had taught me a swear word. She looked pretty surprised and said, "What is the swear word?"

Whispering, I told her, "A-R-S."

I thought that she might be mad but she just smiled. She said, "Well, I wouldn't repeat that to anyone, so we'll keep it a secret just between us, OK?"

That sounded pretty good, but I didn't tell her about all the other swear words that I knew. Maybe she really might get mad. She didn't know about the time that I was mad at Tootsie and told her," I'm calling Dr. Monahan to come down here and give you a shot in your A-R-S."

My cousin Joanie and I had a lot of ear infections and Dr. Monahan would come down with his black bag and check us over. If our ears were infected, he would lay us face down on the living room sofa. He would pat Joanie's butt and say, "Well, this one doesn't have much meat for a shot." Then he would pat my butt and say, "Well, this one has plenty of meat." OK, so I was bigger because I was two weeks older.

Stay tuned for lots more stories.

CHILDREN OF GEORGE AND DELIA ROY

AMEY JOSEPH ROY
7/8/1905 – 9/20/05

AMELIA MARYANNA ROY
4/3/1907 – 4/8/1999

Amelia was a tightly wrapped stick of dynamite. Small and powerful. She married Joseph O'Brien and had four children, John (Jack), Richard (Dick), Mary Letitia, and Phyllis. Her husband Joseph was a boxer. He died young, leaving Amelia alone with four small children. With her strength of character and humor, she did a great job. She was a lot like her mother, Delia Roy. She ruled her house with strength so common in our family. Over the years, she worked as a "nanny" for many families, successfully bringing up well behaved and grateful children and parents. I loved sending her the most tasteless St. Patrick Day and birthday cards every year. She would pretend to be shocked, but I knew that she loved getting them. I sure miss sending those cards. We lost her at the age of eighty-nine. She left a big space in our family.

Jack was the eldest and I recall reading his textbooks when he came home from St. Anslems College where he obtained a teaching degree. He was tall, slim and handsome. He married Geraldine Harney and had five girls.

Dick was the joker in the family. Always a wisecrack and he had the gift of gab. One of his most favorite jobs was owning a bar and being the bartender. He was very active in his hometown of Conway, N.H., enjoyed baseball and had a local park named after him. He was loved and respected.

Letitia was the nurse in the family. She was a supervisor in labor and delivery for many years. She married Milton Rollo and they adopted two children.

Phyllis was named after my mother. She is the quiet one but don't underestimate her. She can move mountains without even raising her voice. She married Lawrence Stinehour and they had four children. For many years, she ran a day care from her home. Her children were happy and well trained by the time they arrived at kindergarten and welcomed by grateful teachers.

Phyllis has been invaluable in her help to compile this memoir. We spent many hours trying to figure out who married who and who was related to who . It took the both of us to recognize many of our ancestors in the hundreds of pictures we inherited.

Amelia Roy O'Brien

AUNT AMELIA'S BLOOMERS

My Aunt Amelia would sometimes look after me and since she had five kids, she was pretty good at making sure I didn't wander away. Her house was right off the main street in town. One afternoon when she was watching me, she decided to wash the kitchen floor. She tucked her skirt into her waistband so it wouldn't get wet. She wore peppermint pink rippled cotton bloomers, gathered just below the knees. When she tucked in her skirt, her bloomers were in plain sight. As she was washing the floor, she suddenly realized that the house was way too quiet.

She jumped up and ran through the house…no Jeannie…out the back door…no Jeannie…so down the street she ran, past Astle's Hardware Store. After a block, she decided to turn back for home. I'll bet by this time she was really mad. As chance would have it, Mr. Astle was standing in the window of his store, and I'll bet that his eyebrows were up to his hairline when he spied Amelia's pink bloomers.

As she entered her front door, she glanced into the shed, and there I was, sitting on the floor trying on my cousin Dick's wading boots.

For years, every time Amelia walked into Mr. Astle's store, he had a grin on his face. She never really forgave me, especially when I retold the story for years at our family reunions.

There were lots of stone walls around the farm and a never ending supply of little garter snakes. I loved playing with them, and I knew that some people were afraid of snakes, especially my aunt Amelia. My chance to scare her came one afternoon when we were playing croquet on the lawn. With a snake curled around my wrist, I tugged on her skirt from behind and raised my hand with the snake so she could see it.

I think that I underestimated what her reaction would be. She began to scream and ran across the lawn, tripping and falling on her face. All the adults came quickly over to her to see if she was hurt. My life was spared since no bones were broken, however, I was given a terrible punishment. I had to sit in the corner for the rest of the afternoon, no books, and no dessert after supper.

The family was relieved when Joanie came down for the day to play with me. We were two peas in a pod and two kids were easier to find than just one. She had five brothers and really liked to come down to the farm. We rode our bikes, checked out the baby pigs, raided Tootsie's rhubarb patch and played with Simone and Bunny. Sometimes Tootsie would give us a little dish of sugar so we could dip our rhubarb in it. When Pa came home from the sawmill, he would take us for a ride on Junie. When Joanie ate supper with us, Pa didn't allow any fooling around at the table. We knew we should be quiet, but the giggles would start. Pa would give us that look, but I think that he smiled sometimes, just a little.

Pa would go to the grain store, with Junie pulling the wagon, to pick up grain and stuff. When there were baby chicks at the store, he would bring some home for Joanie and me. They were put into boxes with sawdust on the bottom and placed next to the wood stove to keep them warm. We sat and watched them for hours but were told not to touch them. When nobody was watching, a tiny finger might be seen reaching out to stroke the soft fur.

My bedroom was over the kitchen and there was a grate in the floor to warm the upstairs. At night, when all the adults were downstairs talking or playing cards, I would lie on the floor with my face on the grate, listening to the rhythm of the words and feeling the warm air. When we had baby chicks, I could hear them chirping. When the house was quiet, I would sneak down the stairs, not stepping on the squeaky stairs, and sit next to the chicks. Disobeying Pa's orders, I would pick up a chick and pet it. They were so cute all sleeping in a pile in the corner of the box and the sawdust smelled so good. I don't think that Pa ever found out about my chick adventures.

Some afternoons were just so boring that I would decide to go up to the laundry to visit Tootsie. I never did find out why they called her Tootsie because her real name was Yvonne. The laundry was always busy because all the big hotels around Whitefield sent all their laundry there. The laundry was way up on the hill near town, just a hop, skip and jump for me. An adventure to break up the day. It was so much fun there with the giant ironing machines like monsters breathing steam. It was easier to let me stay rather than walk me home. Of course, I loved the attention.

I guess these adventures were the reason that my cousins never wanted to babysit me. Many told me at family reunions that I needed two babysitters.

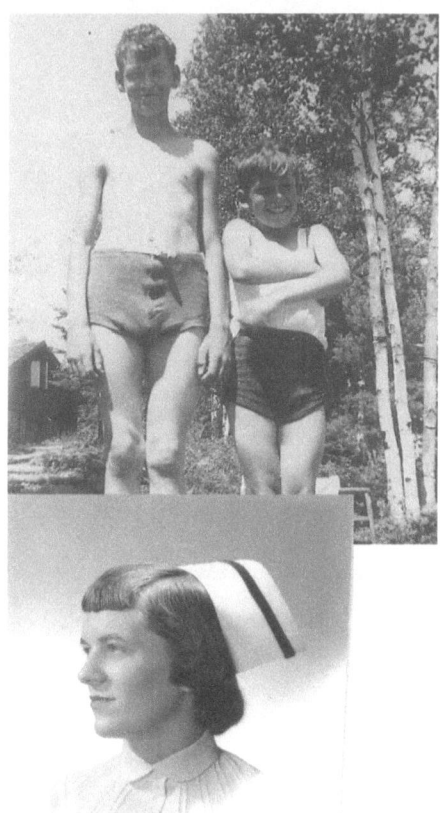

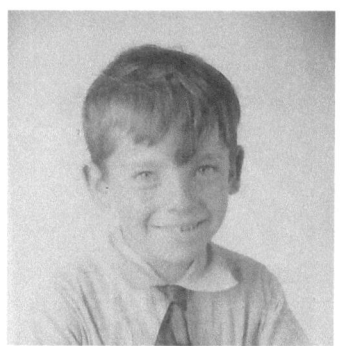

Jack O'Brien

Jack and Dick O'Brien

Letitia O'Brien

Dick O'Brien

Jack O'Brien

Jack and Geraldine Harney
O'Brien in Florida

Letitia O'Brien

Letitia and Milton Rollo

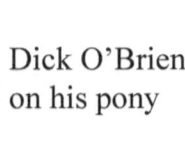

Dick O'Brien
on his pony

Kathy Rollo Kadea,
daughter of Letitia

Patti Jean Stinehour

Phyllis and Letitia O'Brien in front
Dick and Jack O'Brien in back

Phylllis O'Brien Stinehour and
Tootsie Roy

Phyllis O'Brien

GERTRUDE MARIA ROY WILLIAMS
1/20/1909 –

Gertrude attended Plymouth State College and obtained a teaching degree. She married Kenneth Williams and had two children, Carol and Robert. She left New Hampshire and settled with her family in California.

There are many pictures of her and the children at the Water Street farm, but they must have left the area when the children were small.

Emmett and Phyllis traveled to California for a visit and then to Hawaii on vacation with Gertrude and Kenneth. It was the biggest trip my parents ever took and they talked about it for years.

Carol married Fred Doss and also settled in California. Carol raised horses and Fred traveled for his work in laser technology. Fred visited my mother twice in Florida when she was living with me, and she often spoke about how much she appreciated his arranging his schedule to visit with her.

Robert, known as Pudgy, was a baby when I last saw him. He was in the military and after a stroke, has been in rehabilitation in California.

HENRY TIMOTHY (PETE) ROY
3/14/1911 – 6/1/1962

Another Pete! This Pete was also California bound and must have left Whitefield when I was very young. He married Baertha Devoe and they did not have children. Bertha was a happy personality and always loved to visit and talk.

Geraldine Roy in center with friends

Geraldine Roy Williams with Carol and Pudgy Williams and Joan Roy

Carol Williams riding Junie

Geraldine with Carol and Pudgy

Pudgy and Carol Williams

EVA ROY
8/1/1912 – 8/20/1912

Eva was Tootsie's twin sister. They were born before incubators and at home. They were so small that they were placed together on a pillow on the open oven door of the woodstove to keep them warm.

YVONNE TOOTSIE ROY
8/1/1912 – 11/11/2008

Tootsie was the hub of our family. The fact that she outlived all her siblings is testimony to her joy of life and her ability to meet hardship with humor.

She became my second mother when I lived at the farm. In the evenings, Tootsie and I would sit at the maple table and she would patiently play cards with me. We played Flinch, a number game, and this is how I learned my numbers and became an avid card player.

Tootsie never married and never owned a car. When all her siblings left to marry and raise their families, she stayed at home, caring for her parents and the farm. For some people, this may have caused bitterness, but her religious faith and loyalty to her family kept her there. She had an amazing sense of humor and never seemed to get upset. Tootsie was always there, for everyone, and when both her parents were gone, she remained as a resident in Whitefield for all of her ninety-six years.

During those years, we all stopped by to visit, some took her shopping or out to lunch, but mostly, she was our rock. At the age of ninety-two, I talked her into visiting me in Florida. My mother, her sister Phyllis, was not well and was living with me. Tootsie took her first plane ride, her first trip out of New England, and got to dip her feet into the ocean for the very first time.

Her mailman climbed her narrow steep stairs daily to deliver her mail, and for a reward, he got a Kit Kat bar. They also bought lottery tickets together. On the week-ends she watched ice skating or NASCAR. For her ninetieth birthday, I was able to get her a signed poster from her favorite NASCAR driver. She kept that poster on her kitchen wall for all to see.

Her apartment living room was filled with thriving African violets and a vast collection of paperweights. Her granddaughter, Ashley, who played soccer, challenged her to a race up the steep steps. When Ashley turned to see how Tootsie was doing, she was right on her heels. At that time, Tootsie was in her nineties.

I miss giving her those racy love story paperbacks and kidding her about having to go to confession an extra time. She was only four feet and ten inches tall, always in a skirt and short sleeve sweater, knee high nylons, flat shoes, handkerchief in her pocket and a big smile on her face. We lost her at ninety-six years old and we are still looking at each other saying, "Gee, I sure miss Tootsie."

Tootsie and Phyllis Roy

Emmett Shevlin and Tootsie

Tootsie and Phyllis

Tootsie, Phyllis, Cleo

Phyllis Roy Shevlin, Amelia Roy O'Brien,
Yvonne Roy, Gertrude Roy Williams

Gertrude, Tootsie and Phyllis 1988

Tootsie Roy, Bertha Devoe
Roy (Henry's (Pete) wife)
1988

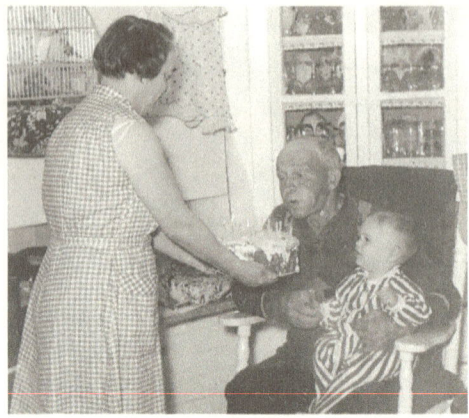

Tootsie, George Roy and baby

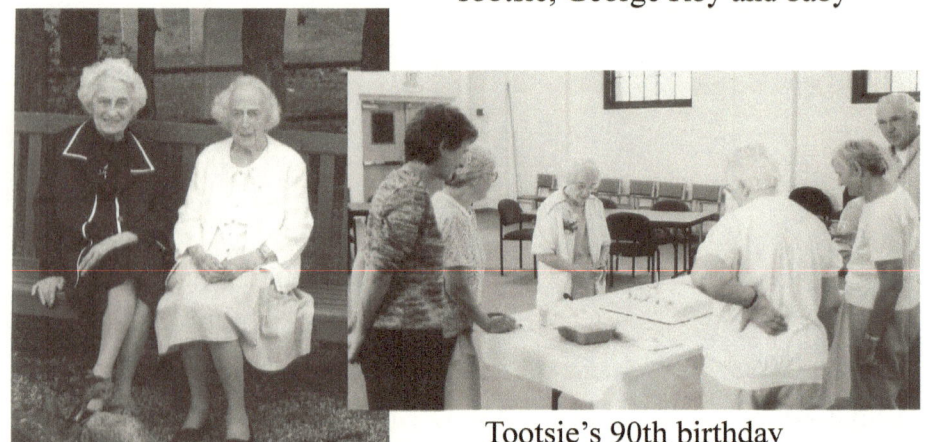

Phyllis and Tootsie

Tootsie's 90th birthday

Amelia Roy O'Brien, Tootsie Roy, Phyllis Roy
Shevlin, Cleo Roy

Back row: Cleo, wife Dolly, George and Delia Roy, Henry (Pete) Roy, Phyllis
Front row: Bertha, Tootsie, Amelia

Emmett and Phyllis Shevlin's wedding picture
Back row: Delia, Phyllis, Emmett, George
Front row: Dolly, Amelia, Bertha and Pete

Back Row: Phyllis O'Brien, Gary Roy, Dick O'Brien, Phillip Roy, Perry Roy, Letitia O'Brien
Front Row: Joan Roy, Jeanne Shevlin

CLEO THOMAS BENTON ROY
2/18/1915 – 8/14/1985

I can still visualize Cleo in mind as if it was yesterday. He was my mother's brother and the father of one of my closest friends, Joanie. He had the same body build as Pa, short, sinewy arms, and a great sense of humor. He played guitar, sang and played some wicked spoons.

Cleo always greeted everyone with a smile, the real kind of smile that crinkled his crow's feet and was reflected in his eyes.

Golf was Cleo's game and beer was Cleo's bane.

One of my fondest memories of Cleo was the day we spent playing golf in Bethlehem, N.H. Due to his cardiac history, he had been advised not to drink or smoke. Of course, he totally ignored all medical advice. After a round of golf, we sat on the deck of the country club, refreshed by ice cold beers, laughed at funny family stories and shared a very special day.

Our next meeting was many years later, at the reception after his funeral. Joanie and I wept, and found comfort in telling tales about her dad. We smiled as her brother, Gary, a golf pro who shared his dad's love of the game, quietly slipped a golf ball into his dad's final resting place.

JOAN ROY BENT
12/31/1942

Joanie and I spent many memorable days at the Water Street farm, riding Junie, jumping from the rafters into the hay, chasing baby pigs and just being kids.

Joanie was shy but friendly, small for her age and always that constant smile that said, "Guess what I'm thinking/" She wasn't as innocent as everyone thought, but some secrets will always remain in the past.

She and Peter were married for over twenty years and seemed the perfect couple and best of friends. Joanie died in her sixties and Peter followed her a few days later.

Cleo Roy on 70th birthday

Cleo

Cleo and Pete

Cleo and Bunny

Joan Roy on Junie with her father, Cleo

Dorothy (Dolly) Pilotte Roy, Cleo's wife

Gary Roy

Joan Roy

Carol Williams and Joan Roy

Cleo with Carol Williams and Joan Roy

Joan Roy

Joan Roy, First Communion

Carol Williams First Communion

MY BARNYARD PLAYMATES

My mom and I are still here at the farm and my dad is coming home soon. She's anxious for him to come home from the war. I'm so excited to see him get off the train but I'm a little scared because I don't remember what he looks like. Mom says "He'll be here in a week," but that is too long for me to wait. I'm still asking her questions about him after we get into bed, and I must have fallen asleep, because it's morning again.

I can smell breakfast cooking downstairs. Mom is still sleeping beside me in bed, so it must be Ma in the kitchen.

"Jeannie. Your pancakes are ready. You'd better get down here before Pa eats them!"

"Don't let him eat my pancakes!" Not taking time to put on a sweater over my pajamas, out of the bed I jump, with Simone, my cat, right behind me. She's been keeping my feet warm all night. It's wintertime and really cold in the house. We both run down the narrow stairs, and I can hear Simone thumping behind me.

"Did Pa eat my pancakes?"

"No, you're lucky that he's still in the barn but you'd better sit down. He's about done and he'll be very hungry."

Simone is patiently waiting by the door that goes out to the shed for her saucer of milk. Ma puts her milk down and we laugh, because we can hear her making squeaky noises and loud purring, like she's saying "Thank you." We don't have any mice in the house or as many rats in the barn because Ma says she's a "good mouser". Simone leaves uneaten pieces of rats at our back door. Ma says she's leaving us "gifts" because she loves us. I think it's scary to see rat heads and feet.

Pa comes stomping in from the barn, shaking the snow off his boots on the rug. He doesn't smile very much and sometimes I don't know if he's kidding me or mad. Bunny, our black and white collie is right behind him, where he usually is. Pa says that Bunny is his sidekick, like Roy Rogers and Trigger.

"Are my pancakes done? Don't tell me that Jeannie ate them all or I'll have to put her over my knee. (I look at Ma to see if she's smiling.) All the water in the barn froze over last night and I had to lug buckets of water from the stream to the barn. I'm so hungry I could eat a horse!"

I know he doesn't mean Junie, our horse. He's smiling a little so I guess he's just kidding me again. Junie works with him every day at the saw mill so he takes really good care of her like a best friend.

Pa finishes his breakfast, drinks up his coffee and puts on his coat to go to work. Bunny is chasing his tail in circles and barking because he's excited to go to work with Pa and Junie.

Ma clears up the dishes, leaving a place set for my mom. She'll be getting up soon to go to work as a telephone operator .

Ma says, "Go upstairs and wake your mom up. As soon as you're dressed, it's time for your hair."

I know what she means about my hair. Ma is the only one that can stand the screaming as I get my long hair brushed. Up the stairs and I jump on the bed. My mom is already awake and has all my clothes out. I'm not in a big hurry, but my mom needs to go to work, so I get dressed really fast and run back down the stairs. I like to run everywhere.

"Assiez vous!".I know this means to sit down. Ma sometimes gives me orders in French and I can't make believe that I don't know what she's saying. She's not afraid to use the yardstick. The usual screaming stops as all the snarls in my hair are combed out. The tears dry as she braids my hair. Shoes and socks are put on and I'm ready for the day. If this sound like I'm spoiled, I guess I am because all my cousins say so.

Finally, one day mom says my dad is coming home tomorrow.

"OK Jeannie, we're going to meet your dad at the train station at ten o'clock in the morning so you have to go to bed early." This is one night that I don't have to be asked twice to go up to bed.

The minute I wake up, I know the special day is here. I am downstairs in a flash for breakfast.

While Ma was making breakfast she says, "Jeannie, would you like to wear one of your special Sunday dresses today?"

"Oh, could I? Can I wear the yellow ones with the ruffles?" Ma makes all my dresses, and the ruffled ones are special.

This morning, nobody has to help me get washed and dressed. I'm done in a blink, except for a few buttons and putting on my shoes. Soon, Ma is braiding my hair while I squirm. Not a peep today. No crying.

My mom, Ma Pa, and Tootsie and I are ready to go at last. We all head up to the train station on Main Street. We don't have long to wait until we hear the train engine tooting.

As people get off, I start to run. "Daddy, Daddy!" I run as fast as I can because I know who he is. He picks me up and hugs me and I start to ask him lots of questions. Everyone is watching us and lots of people are crying. I don't know why they are crying because I'm really happy.

My mom finally gets a hug too and he hugs everyone, even Pa.

He smiles at my mom and asks her, "Did she get vaccinated with a phonograph needle?"

After my Dad came home, he helps Pa do lots of chores around the farm. One of my chores is to get Junie in the pasture and bring her into the barn for her supper. First I have to go into the barn to get her harness with the clip on the end. Pa showed me which one, so I could do it alone after that. I walk down our dirt road, past Maudie's house, turn left at the stop sign and then down the road to the pasture. I leave the gate open so I can ride her out. Junie is a giant work horse and I am always afraid that if I get too close, she'll step on my toes with her metal shoes.

"Come on big girl, I'm here to take you home." I talk very softly to her and I think she knows who I am. Slowly, I get closer and clip the harness under her long chin, and lead her to the fence. Climbing up on the fence, I slide onto her wide back. She is so warm from the sunshine and she smells like horse sweat and hay. Getting a handful of her long white hair on her neck, I make a clicking sound with my tongue. Giving her a gentle kick in her belly, we're off for home. Junie knows the way and she never runs, but walks slowly all the way to the barn where she knows that Pa has her supper waiting.

I also play a lot with Bunny. He has long black and white silky hair and a long nose. When he wants me to throw his ball, he pokes me on my leg with his nose. We play on the front lawn. He chases me and I chase him. One Sunday afternoon, after Mass and Sunday dinner, everyone was out on the porch visiting. Bunny is chasing me around as usual. He suddenly jumps on me, pushing me down on the grass. Then he falls over and doesn't move.

My Mom runs really fast and picks me up. I'm not even crying. She brushes the grass of my clothes, and checks me over. I don't hurt at all but when I look at Bunny, I start crying.. He's making little whimpering noises and there is lots of blood on his belly fur. Pa picks him up and carries him to the wagon my dad had harnessed up, and Pa and my dad take him to the vet.

We're all waiting on the porch for what feels like a long time and soon, Pa and the wagon are coming down the road.

"Is Bunny going to be OK?" I am near the wagon and can see that Bunny has a big white bandage on his belly.

Bunny is smiling, I know he is. I can tell. He's happy to be home. "What did the doctor say, Pa?"

Pa said, "The vet said Bunny had been shot but the bullet didn't go deep. He thought that maybe someone in a nearby field had been shooting and the bullet went into our yard.

Pa carries Bunny into the kitchen and lays him down on a blanket near the stove. I get him a bowl of water and sit next to him to keep him company.

That night at supper, Pa told us that dogs can hear things that people can't hear. He said, "Maybe Bunny heard a gun go off and pushed Jeannine down to protect her."

That's how Bunny became my hero dog.

Just when I'm having such a good life, one day my mom and dad bring home a baby. They say he's my baby brother and his name is Ralph. I take one look at him and say, "Take him back. I don't want him." Everyone is saying what a beautiful baby he is, and I'm not sure I like him getting so much attention.

Soon after my baby brother Ralph came to live with us, my life changes even more. It is time for us to move to Berlin, about thirty miles away, where my dad will be working as an electrician at the paper mill. We move into an apartment in Berlin Mills on 6th Street. Soon it will be time for me to start the first grade in the fall. We still have the summer to spend time at the farm on week-ends when dad has days off.

A big deal in the summer is when it's time to cut the hay and put in into the barn hay loft for Junie to eat in the winter. It is an exciting week-end and the whole family gets involved.

"Jeannie, are you excited about going to Whitefield this week-end? I think your cousin Joanie will be staying with us at the farm. Won't that be fun?"

My mom is packing my play clothes and getting my baby brother Ralph ready, too. He has to come everywhere. We'll be cutting the hay in Maudie's back yard. Maudie has a big hayfield, and when the time is just right, all my uncles, cousins, Pa, and my Dad get ready to cut the grass. All the ladies and girls stay at Maudie's and make lunch and lemonade. It's the girls' job to take water out to the men while they are cutting the grass.

First the grass is cut with long knives called scythes. Then Junie is hitched up to a rake like a giant comb behind two wheels and a seat. Pitchforks are used to turn the hay until it dries. By the next day, it s ready to be loaded into the hay wagon. Poor Junie does most of the really hard work. First she pulls the rake and then has to pull the hay wagon.

My cousin, Joanie and I love to join all the men and boys (four boys are her brothers), and try to pitch as much hay as they can up into the hay wagon. We hate to be outdone by boys.

"Hey, Joanie, are you ready to help clean up? We can't go jumping in the hay until Maudie's house is clean and everything is put away." I'm getting really impatient.

My mom knows how anxious we are to get our reward for working hard the past two days. We're looking forward to jumping from the rafters into the hay.

"You girls go ahead and have fun. No fighting!" She knows that Joanie's four brothers plus a whole bunch of kids will be there.

By this time, the hay loft is pretty full and all the kids are in the barn. We're all pushing for first place, and climbing the rafters into the highest part of the barn. It sure feels like we're going to jump a mile down into the hay. Well, maybe not a mile, but it seems like a mile when you are screaming on that first jump down. Joanie and I scream with the rest of them, but push our way into the line to jump again.

As my life revolves from farm to city, it is time to start school. My new school allows me to start at the age of five, so I don't have to go to kindergarten. I can't wait to learn to read better,   (I can already read books by myself) and to make new friends.

Emmett, Jeanne, and Bunny

BERLIN, NEW HAMPSHIRE

Berlin was chartered in 1829, and remained settled only by farmers until the realization that the power of the Androscoggin River, which ran through the town, could be harnessed and used for manufacturing. In the mid 1800's, a sawmill was built there by a group of businessmen and papermaking mills were built along the banks of the Androscoggin River, later to be known as The Brown Paper Company. The mill soon attracted immigrants to the area, many from Canada. The town and the Brown Company both grew over the years, and by the 1950,s, there were about 15,000 people living in Berlin. When driving into the city, the large tortuous river could be seen snaking its way down through the valley, the hills on either side of the river were shaped like a bowl with houses glued to its sides. You had to be part mountain goat to live in Berlin. Everywhere you lived, it was uphill. Strangers to town would begin to notice an odor of rotten eggs about 5 miles away, an unfortunate by product of paper mills.

Our town was a great place to live in the 1940's and 50's. Main Street was thriving with businesses, it was safe for kids to walk to school, we hung out at the 5&10 cent store for cherry cokes and French fries after school, to the movies or the library, to the community center for swimming lessons, or just ride our bikes on the streets near our homes. For years, there was a large hockey stick with HOCKEY TOWN, USA, hanging over the entrance of Main Street. Berlin had a great hockey team and we spent lots of time at the Berlin Arena for hockey games and open skating in the winter and roller skating the rest of the year. Since the area had so much snowfall, it was a popular place for skiing, and Berlin hosted the international ski jump competitions at the Nansen Ski Jump in Milan.

My parents lived in Berlin after they were married, my mother and I moved to Whitefield when my Dad was stationed in Korea, and then back to Berlin when he returned. Since the mill was the biggest employer, my Dad worked there as an electrician, as his father had years ago. During my Dad's early years at the Cascade branch of the paper mill, he completed a correspondence course to be a licensed electrician. He remained at the same mill until his retirement at 65.

The Paleo-indians mined rhyolite in the Jasper Caves in Berlin to make tools. This mine is the only prehistoric archeological site on the National Register of Historic Places in the United States. My uncle, Morris Wheeler, lived in Milan, just outside Berlin, and had a large collection of arrowheads, reflecting the many Indian residents in our area in the past.

Berlin Main Street 1967

Hockey Town USA 1967

Brown Paper Company

ENDURING PAROCHIAL SCHOOL

My mom, dad and baby brother Ralph and I had just moved from the farm in Whitefield to Berlin. We had a new apartment on 6th Street in Berlin Mills and my dad would be starting his new job at the Cascade Paper Mill soon. I was really excited about being in the first grade. All his family had gone to St. Kieran's school and church and Monsignor Walsh was a family friend. There wasn't any doubt about where I would be going to school.

Soon the day arrived and at five years old, I was waiting for my first ride on a school bus. Excited about my new uniforrm and shoes, and with my schoolbag over my shoulder, mom and I waited for the school bus at the corner of our street.

As she walked me to the bus stop, she gave me a big hug and said, "Now Jeannie, remember the bus number so you can find the same bus to bring you home."

Being so excited, I was only half listening. As I looked up and saw the big #2 on the side of the bus, I repeated, "I'll get on the #2 bus when I get out of school."

Nervously climbing the giant steps into the bus, it was filled with kids jumping around, yelling to friends. I'd never seen kids act this way. Quietly I slid into the first open seat. When I arrived at my school, kids were lining up outside the buses. The nuns had the boys in one line, girls in another line. I followed the girl in front of me like follow the leader as we all entered the giant red brick building.

The Sisters of Mercy wore dresses that were frightening, like big black and white monsters. I wondered if they had any hair under that big thing on their heads. They wore a wide black belt with giant rosary beads hanging down. The heels of their black shoes clicked on the floor of the hallway when they walked. All the nuns looked the same. It was hard to tell which nun it was.

"Children, my name is Sister Mary Bernadine and I'll be your teacher. You must sit in your seat and pay attention to what I say. If you have a question or need to go to the bathroom, you must raise your hand."

"Yes Sister", we all answered together and loudly.

The sister made a cricket sound from her hand. When she made that noise, we would sit, stand, go, stop, or pray. We had to learn a lot of prayers. It was good that we said the same ones over and over because it was easier to remember the words.

Sister Bernadine smiled a lot but she was very strict. We had homework on the first night. Letter pictures hung above the blackboard, starting with "a". We had to fill a whole page with little "a" letters and bring it back the next day. If we did a good job, we got a star on the top of the homework. I really wanted a star to bring home to show my mom and dad.

That first day was filled with learning how to sit quietly in our seat, learning prayers, but the best part was when Sister Bernadine read us a story about Jesus. I even got a star on my "a" letters and couldn't wait to show my parents. The day went by really fast. Everyone lined up to get on buses. I walked up and down the sidewalk, looking at all the numbers on the side of the buses, but I couldn't find #2 anywhere. Not knowing what to do, I just picked a bus, hoping that it was going by my street. I took a seat near a window so I could see my street. The bus driver let kids get off and pretty soon I was the last one on the bus. The bus driver noticed me sitting all alone. I began crying.

"What's your name?" asked the bus driver.

"My name is Jeannie Shevlin and I think I got on the wrong bus."

"Is Emmett your Dad?

"Yes, Emmett is my Dad. Do you know where he lives?"

"Don't you worry because I know exactly what house you live in and I'll take you right home." The bus driver was so nice, I thought.

Of course, by the time I got home it was getting dark and my Mom was very worried. When she saw the school bus pull up, she ran out to the sidewalk. As the bus door opened, I flew out and into her arms, sobbing. I was so glad to be home. That was my last bus ride. I was driven to school from that day on.

By second grade I was ready to make my first communion, a big event in our family. I had to learn lots of catechism in books before I could wear my beautiful new white dress and walk down to the altar and take communion. It was a piece of bread that only the priest could touch. He put it on our tongue and then we could swallow it. Before we could make our first communion, we had to make our first confession. We couldn't have any sins on our souls when we ate the communion, so we had to tell all our sins first. Sins were a big thing with the sisters. There were big sins and little sins and it seemed like everything was a sin. There was even a list of ten commandment sins we had to learn. If we were bad it meant that we would go to Hell. This was very scary so we didn't dare commit sins because we would have to stay in the fires of Hell forever.

On the Saturday before the Sunday First Communion, I had to go to confession for the first time. It was a dark box, where I sat on one side of the wall and the priest sat on the other side and we talked though a little window. It was like being in a warm blanket and smelled like candles. I didn't know how many times I had lied, disobeyed my parents or any other sins on the list. I knew I hadn't killed anybody but some of the other sins I didn't understand. So, I thought about the biggest number I could think of and told the priest that I had committed one hundred of everything. The priest didn't answer right away. Finally he said "My child, for your penance say five Hail Marys and five Our Fathers."

My second, third and fourth grade sisters were nice. I didn't like not being able to talk, laugh, or move around in the classroom. I also didn't like all the praying and having to march two by two up to the church to say some more prayers.

Sometimes we had to say hundreds of prayers around and around the beads of the whole rosary.

There were some fun things during elementary school. When I was in the third grade, my mother let me take tap and ballet classes. Dancing was so much fun. At night I would dream about wearing real ballet shoes, a tutu, and being a famous ballerina. One night when my dad was sitting in his chair reading his paper after work, I was practicing my arabesques back and forth in the living room. He watched a few of my moves and said, "That's it, young lady. No more money on ballet lessons. You're as graceful as a cow on roller skates."

My dad agreed that I could continue tap lessons. I have lots of pictures of our recitals and costumes. Because I learned a dance by watching another student, I was asked to do her solo dance when she got sick. It was a rumba and the costume was a ruffled dress split up the thigh. I still secretly wished that I could have been a ballerina.

In the fifth grade, my life changed drastically. My teacher was Sister Frances. She was known as a teacher who hit children. My cousin got hit so many times on the neck he got big sores.

"Mom, do I have to stay in that school? I hate it there. That Sister Frances is so mean to everyone. Nobody likes her."

"Jeannie, we knew when you started that grade that she wasn't a very nice nun, but your father says that you can't change schools. This year will be over before you know it."

One afternoon, Sister Frances called me to the front of the class.

"Class, I want to show you what happens when you don't study for a test. This is Miss Shevlin's math score – 56. Miss Shevlin, please hold out your hands, palms up."

Even though I knew it was coming, the three slaps from the ruler on my palms hurt. There was no way that Sister Frances would see my cry. I sat down in my seat, so embarrassed that she made fun of me in front of the whole class.

That night, when my dad came home from work, I told him," I'm never returning to that school again and no matter what you do to me, I'll never go back." I even dreamed about running away from home but I didn't know where I would go.

When he and my Mom discussed what happened, it was agreed that my Mom would go to the school to speak with Sister Frances. When my mom asked her what happened, she denied slapping me. My mom knew that I was not lying. It was decided that night that I would not have to go back to St. Kieran's. When Monsignor Walsh found out I left the school, he even came to our house. My Dad told him, "Jeannie would not lie about what happened and she will be going to the public school."

I was enrolled in Bartlett School, the public school near my house. I loved it there, and never missed St. Kieran's, not even once. We could talk in class, laughed with the teachers, and had fun at recess .My fifth grade was the best year I ever had. At the end of every school day, Miss Wilson read us a chapter of a book, my favorite book being WHITE FANG. I even won every spelling bee.

This was the same year that I took up the trombone. My dad wasn't too happy when I took it out and began to practice. I had to blow really hard to get any noise and the sounds that came out were not music.

"Jeannie, I'm sorry but you'll have to return the trombone to school. It makes too much noise and the neighbors will complain."

That was my very short trombone career. My mom felt so bad that she agreed that I could take piano lessons. I think my parents thought I might be good at something but they just hadn't found out what it was yet. I guess ballet and trombones were on the list of things I wasn't good at.

Miss Willa was our town piano teacher. She lived in an old gingerbread house on High Street with her mother. The house was so old and creaky that it looked kind of haunted. Kids were seen coming and going after school hours and on Saturday. I learned how to hold my hands, beginner scales, twinkle- twinkle little star, and soon began to learn some classical music pieces.

At the beginning of each lesson, I would beg for a private concert. Willa would pull her bench up to the immense black piano, sit up very straight, raise her arms, and bring her hands down on the keys. The melody of Tchaikovsky's Concerto in B Flat Minor would fill the house. I loved that music, never having heard such sounds before. When I heard that musicI felt good all over. During lessons, there would be a faint ringing sound, and she would go upstairs to take care of her mother. I used to think how sad it was that she couldn't leave home and be a concert pianist. After many years of lessons, although I was never a gifted piano player, she taught me to appreciate classical music.

Our town was small and very safe. We rode our bikes or played tag in the streets until dark. Our parents could be heard calling us in to take a bath and get ready for bed. We lived on Jolbert Street and it was full of kids. The neighborhood families were close and many times we all went on summer outings. Cedar Pond was only about twenty miles away and we would load up and away we would go for swimming and cook-outs. The kids loved to talk our parents into playing baseball and it became a free for all, yelling, sliding into bases, and hoping it was our dad who hit a home run.

Some of the lakes had outdoor bathrooms called outhouses. All of us kids told stories about how you could get bitten on the butt by a spider hiding under the wooden seat inside the outhouse. I always checked really good before I sat down. Nope, I never had a bite but the smell made your eyes cry. After the first time using the outhouse, I learned that you'd better bring your own toilet paper. It was better than using the old phone book with torn out pages that somebody left in there.

The summers passed so quickly and soon it was time to begin the seventh grade at Berlin High School. Grades seven to twelve were in the same building. I couldn't wait to go to school with the older kids. I could pick some of my own classes, make new friends, and go to dances with boys.

Dance recital, Jeanne center with rumba costume

Jeanne Shevlin
First Communion

Jeanne with the "sisters"

THE FAMILY OF EMMETT PATRICK SHEVLIN

Robert Shevlin (1806) relative from Queenstown,
   Cork County, Ireland
Willliam Murphy (1841) married Mary Alice Condon..
   (Emmett Shevlin's great grandfather)
Cornelius Edward Murphy (1874) father of Patrick Murphy

Robert Murphy married Mary Cullen and had six children
   Mildred (1907 -1974) married Albert Wheeler (1911 – 1984) and had five children
      Albert – no marriageMonica (1933 – 1968) – no marriage
      Morris married Bea Tanguay and had four children,
         Jay, Jill, Jayne and Joel
      Donny married Gert Lheureux and had nine children
      Joan married ___Lamarre and had four children,
         Brian, Bess, Bonnie and Brad
   Michael married Faith Hickey – no children
   Robert married Dorothy Tourangeau and had two children
      Colleen married William Phinney and had four children,
         Glen, Duane, John, and Maria
   Cullen married Mary Murphy (2015) and had three children, Eileen, Colleen and Maureen
      Eileen married Chris Schmeke and had two children,
         Jareth and Ben
      Colleen married David Harper and had one child,
         Sean
      Colleen married ___and had one child, Matthew
      Maureen – no marriage

Raymond married Dorothy McDonald and had one child
  Lynn married Gary Pinette and had one child,
  Kim
Henry married ___ and had two children
  Frances married ____ and had two children
  Howard (Ducky) married ____ and had four children,
    Linda, Mary, Michael and Bobby
Mary (1896 – 1931) married Patrick Shevlin and had five children
  Ralph (1919 – 1931) died at age sixteen
  Emmett Shevlin (4/16/17 – 12/10/81) married Phyllis Roy and had two children,
    Jeanne and Ralph
  Joyce (1917 – 4/30/00) married John Noyes and had one child
    Shanna married ____ Harrison and had five children
  Robert married Doris ____ and had two children,
    Doris Joyce and Robert Jr.
  Warren John married Pauline Strout and had one son
    Michael married Monique Adjami

THE CHILDREN OF PATRICK AND MARY SHEVLIN

RALPH SHEVLIN
1917 – 1931

Ralph was born in Berlin and died at the age of sixteen from a ruptured appendix.

JOYCE SHEVLIN
8/12/22 – 4/30/00

Joyce was very close to Emmett. While they lived with their grandmother, Mary, she helped in the house and the boys slept in the shed beside the house. Despite her rocky start, Joyce always had a positive attitude and a personality that fit in anywhere. Joyce inherited the sense of humor so common in our family. I treasure the time I spent with her. In high school, often I was called Joyce by the teachers who had known her in the past and saw such a resemblance between us.

She married John Noyes from Randolph, N.H. and they traveled a great deal. They settled in Port Huron, Mi. They had one daughter, Shanna. Shanna graduated from nursing school and married a physician, settling in Iowa with their five children.

ROBERT SHEVLIN

Robert married Doris ____ and had two children, Doris and Robert Jr. They settled in Lake Wales, Fl.

WARREN JOHN SHEVLIN
1921 – 2002

John married Pauline Strout and adopted her son, Michael.

Emmett Shevlin   Ralph Shevlin,

Ralph's confirmation or high school graduation

Joyce Shevlin

Joyce Shevlin Noyes with daughter Shanna and ?

Joyce and Shanna

Joyce and John Noyes

Joyce, Jeanne Shevlin Gates, John

Warren and wife Pauline, Phyllis, Emmett, Doris and Robert Shevlin, Robert Jr. and little Doris

Doris and Robert Jr.

Doris, little Doris, Robert

Emmett Shevlin, Warren (John)

Coleen Murphy   Cullen and Coleen are children of Dot and Robert

Henry Murphy – Emmett Shevlin's uncle

Cullen Murphy, Ralph Shevlin, Dot and Robert Murphy

Raymond Murphy uncle of Emmett Shevlin, and brother of Robert

Emmett, Jeanne,
Cullen, Coleen,
Robert, Dot

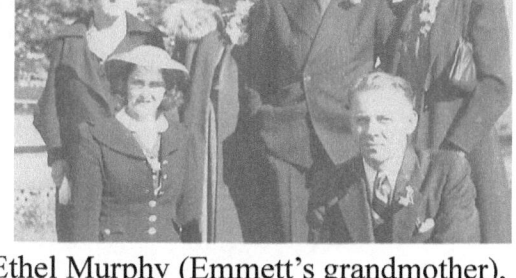

Back Row: Ethel Murphy (Emmett's grandmother),
Phyllis, Emmett, Dot Murphy (Robert Murphy's wife)
Front row: Joyce Shevlin Noyes, Robert Murphy

Emmett, Jeanne, ?, Dot and Raymond Murphy
with daughter, Lynn

Joyce Shevlin Noyes with
Joan Wheeler, her niece,
daughter of Albert Wheeler

The Wheeler family, Milan N.H.

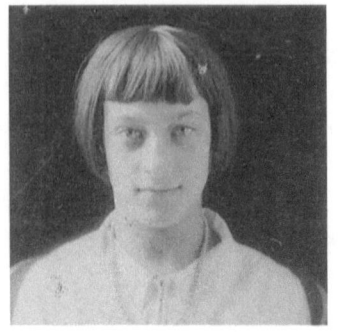
Phyllis Roy

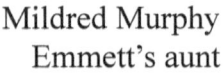
Mildred Murphy
Emmett's aunt

Phyllis and Emmett

Dolly, Bertha and Phyllis

Emmett and Phyllis

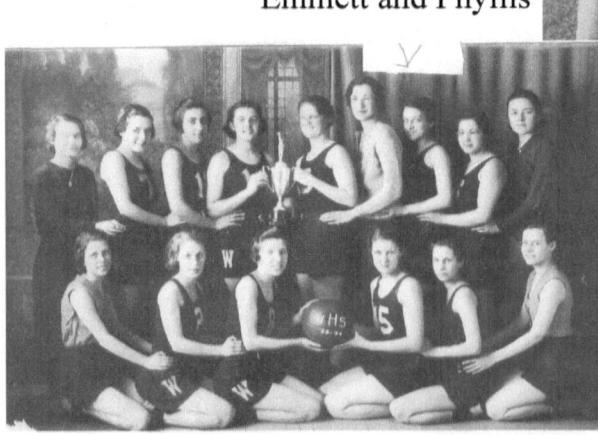
Phyllis Roy on basketball team

Phyllis Roy's graduation from Whitefield High School, first class to graduate from that school

Phyllis and Jeanne

Phyllis

Phyllis and Jeanne

Phyllis and Tootsie

PHYLLIS EIRLEEN ROY SHEVLIN
7/24/1917 – 7/5/2006

Phyllis was the youngest of all the Roy children and was nicknamed "Baby", but you'd better not call her that to her face.

My mom had "the look" down pat. When you got that blazing eye contact, whatever you were doing, you stopped immediately. If you were not near eye contact, you got all four names, like "Ralph Emmett Patrick Shevlin." Of course, my mother never had to use all four names on me because I was always the perfect child, just ask my baby brother, Ralph.

She was a strict disciplinarian and we didn't get away with much. Like her mother, Delia Roy, she ran her home with a firm hand. Everyone who met her would describe her as a very quiet person, spare with words, soft spoken and kind. All those things were very true but there was another Phyllis, who as I became older and a little wiser, I could see down deep. She was the child that should have been college educated. She would, with ease, do crosswords, answer every question on TV shows, help us with our homework no matter what subject, and helped my dad obtain his correspondence course electrical license.

She was a stay at home mom until we entered high school and then worked as a telephone operator. Later, she worked in offices in town and was always promoted to positions of authority. She was another "rock" in the Roy family and we were the lucky ones to have her.

When it was time to have a funeral for her, the local priest didn't know her since she had been living with me in Florida. The priest said to Ralph and I, "Tell me about your mother." We told him, "We never in our life ever heard our mother say a bad word about anybody." As mothers go, she was the best. She raised two children who were never arrested, never used drugs or embarrassed the family. I must admit that I pushed the envelope on that last one. Ralph and I have worked hard, earned an education after high school, had careers, raised our families and have our parents to thank for showing us how to be good people.

We miss her every day.

Emmett in front of Quonset hut in Korea

Sgt. Emmett Shevlin, U.S. Army

Emmett

Emmett and Jeanne on Junie

Emmett and Phyllis

Emmett with Jeanne and Ralph at farm

Emmett

Emmett and Phyllis on right –
on leave in Georgia

EMMETT PATRICK SHEVLIN
4/16/1917 – 12/10/1981

Emmett was the fourth of five children, who lost his father at the age of five and his mother at the age of sixteen. All five children were raised by a grandmother who was not equipped to raise all these children during the depression. Life for them was more than difficult and this poverty left scars never fully erased.

Had I known my father during his teens, he would have been one of those handsome "bad boys" that girls love so much. He was charming, funny, a good dancer, had a crooked smile and was a hard worker. Because he didn't own a car, when he was courting my mother he would hop the train in Berlin and get off in Whitefield. They would go to the dances at Forest Lake. My Mom said that once he came down to the farm for the week-end and ended up staying six weeks.

Emmett finished high school and soon after marrying Phyllis, he served as a Sergeant in the U.S.Army. Upon returning from the military in Korea, he earned his electrician license and was employed at the Cascade Paper Mill until his retirement at sixty-five. His vacations every summer were spent with the family, going on short trips. One of my favorites was visiting his Army buddy in Deer Isle, Me. He was a lobster fisherman and these trips were always filled with adventures, like the time I fell into their open cesspool from outdoor plumbing.

Looking back on my childhood, he was what fathers were supposed to be. Not perfect, but always there, sitting in his chair after work, reading the newspaper until supper was ready, and supper at 5:30 sharp. You'd better not be late. We had the same menu every night, same thing, same day, like beans, brown bread and hot dogs on Saturday night. I hated beans and until this day, they make me nauseous just to look at them. It wasn't until adulthood that I realized that there were more than four vegetables and some people put sauce on their food. I don't recall eating at a restaurant except on vacation.

As a father, he was the monster who chased us around the house with his false teeth out, asked us to pull his finger, (you know that one), and tried to kiss us when he had shaving foam on his face. He was the dad who sat out on the front porch at night and gave all the neighborhood kids a nickel to go up to Gagne's on the corner to buy a popsicle. I loved it when there was a wedding with dancing so I could watch my parents show off their great dancing skills.

His work ethic left an indelible impression on me and my brother. My brother got his good looks and I got his sense of humor.

JEANNE PATRICIA ANN SHEVLIN GATES
12/11/1942 –

I was born at the St. Louis Hospital in Berlin, N.H. If I could have picked a time to have lived in Berlin, I think this was a great era in the 40's and 50's. Life was bustling, the mill was employing lots of locals, there were stores all up and down Main Street, a movie theater, bowling alley, community center, three high schools, and generally things were good.

The data in this book was collected because I wanted my children, grandchildren and interested relatives to know what life was like back "in the old days".

Think about not having television, cell phones or any phone at all, computers, electric washers and dryers, only manual shifts in cars, rare airplane travel, cartoons before the main movie, walking to school or to hang out with friends, riding your bicycle while still in high school, or having to work for an allowance of one to five dollars a week.

We thought life was great back then. I still do.

I hope that this glimpse into my life will enrich the lives of those who read this and being back some good memories to those who lived during these years.

St. Louis Hospital   Berlin, N.H.

Jeanne Shevlin

Jeanne showing off one of Ma's handmade dresses

Jeanne and Ralph

Phyllis, Jeanne and Emmett

Emmett and Jeanne at train station in Berlin

Easter Parade dance in third grade at St. Kieran's Elementary

The "line up" in ballet, Jeanne 5th from left

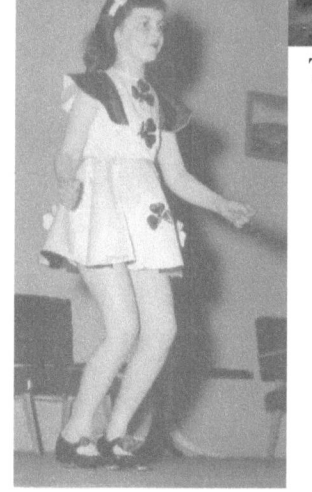

Jeanne tap dancing at the St. Patrick's Day celebration at St. Matthew's

Ralph visiting Jeanne at Girl Scout camp in Gorham, N.H. ?girl on left

Bartlett Elementary School

Jeanne – high school

Jeanne and tenor sax in Brown Paper Company uniform

Jeanne – high school graduation

SKATING DAYS

What a change from sixth grade to junior high school. Berlin High School had grades seven to twelve in the same building so our class was the youngest. I was in awe of the older kids. Would I ever get to be a senior?

I could actually pick some of my classes and this was when I had to start making decisions about what I was going to do after high school. Since my parents always talked about how I should become a nurse like my cousins, I thought that I'd better take classes that would get me admitted to a nursing school.

"Hey, JoJo. Since you, Jeanne Ann, Raynette, Carole and Patti are all taking secretarial classes, I think that I'll take them , too."

"What? Jeannie, are you nuts or something? When you decide to become a secretary?"

"Well, you and the gang want to go to Boston to secretarial school after graduation and that sounds like fun. If I don't get into nursing school I'd love to live in Boston and we would have a ball there. I went to a baseball game there with my parents. We visited my uncle who lives in Boston and it's a great city and far away from Berlin."

It was settled. I enrolled in typing, shorthand and all the other classes that were required for a secretary. In addition, I took chemistry, French, and all the other stuff I needed for nursing school. Good thing that the secretary courses didn't require any homework, but then, I never took home much homework anyway.

I had to learn how to type on a Remington typewriter. I wasn't a very good or fast typist and made lots of mistakes. If we needed a copy of our typing, we had to put a piece of carbon paper between the pages. That meant, when I made a mistake, I had to correct it on both copies. What a drag.

Uniforms were not required at our school but girls could not wear long pants and your skirt better be below the knee or you were sent home to change. Our skirts were puffed out by crinoline petticoats, layers of them, soaked in sugar solution and dried on the clothesline. It made out skirts swish when we walked. What a messy job, soaking net petticoats in a tub of hot sugar water and then carrying them out to the clothesline without making a mess form the dripping sugar. We also wore sweaters with attachable collars, some made of angora yarn. Because Pat Boone was popular, so were suede shoes. Sock hops got their name from the long socks we wore, twisted around and around, that we wore while dancing without shoes.

On Tuesday and Thursday nights and Sunday afternoons, we always wore our puffy skirts roller skating.

"Linda, are you and the gang going roller skating Tuesday night?"

"Sure, Jeannie, want to meet at my house at 6:30? We'll all hang out for a while then walk down to the arena about 7."

When I got there, some of the girls had chipped in to buy a pack of cigarettes for 25 cents. They were sitting on the couch in the living room, feet up on the coffee tables, smoking and drinking cokes. I could almost see their underwear with the crinoline skirts puffed up in the air, legs handing out.

"Hi, Jeannie, want a cigarette?" Linda was so cool and popular. I really wanted to fit in so I said, "Sure, I'll have one."

I wasn't about to tell anyone that when I hung out with my other group of friends, I never had smoked. Taking a cigarette and lighting it up, I inhaled and did not expect the awful taste. A couple more small l puffs and I began to feel the effects. I became so dizzy and when my head began to spin, I felt like throwing up. Sipping on my coke, I just held the cigarette without taking another puff. After a while, I felt a little better and nobody had noticed that I hadn't been smoking.

"OK gang. let's head out", Linda yelled. With Linda in the lead, we all grabbed our metal cases with our roller skates and took the short walk to the arena.

The arena had an organ player who played all the popular songs. When we got there, it would be open skating before the numbers began. The numbers were special dances the good skaters learned. That meant a boy asking you to skate. There were numbers that partners turned and turned to the music and some that everyone skated backwards. If I was lucky, a boy would ask me to dance, a reason to learn all the dances.

In the winter there was ice skating at the arena and attending high school hockey games. We had a hockey rivalry between Berlin High School and Notre Dame High School. The games were so exciting and we all went home hoarse from yelling for our team. Somehow the boys at the other school seemed more handsome and unavailable.

Our town was called "Hockey Town, U.S.A." and in addition to the high school teams, there were adult games when teams from Canada came down to play our local teams. It seems like every neighborhood had a skating rink where we would hang out in sub zero temperatures after school and at night, skating until we couldn't stand the cold any longer. Why did we hang out there? It was because that's where the boys were!

I had a group of best friends, Jeanne Anne, JoJo, Patty, Raynette, Carole, Peggy and Carolyn. Some were from grade school and some were new from high school. We were all so different it was amazing that we all got along so well. We hung out at Carole's house and everyone brought their newest 45's and played them on Carole's record player. The Everly Brothers, Chubby Checker, Ricky Nelson and many others were popular. If we knew how to do the dances they were doing on American Bandstand, we practiced in Carole's room upstairs. We probably shook the whole house. Later, we would make pizzas. Some of the girls drank beer or hard liquor. These had the same effect on me as smoking. I neither smoked nor drank in high school and it seemed that all through high school I was always the one driving.

Our town was kind of insulated from the rest of the world. We heard about rockets going to the moon with people in them, and the cold war with Russia. We didn't have any racial problems like we read in the papers. There were no black people in our town. We didn't have any newspaper articles about bad things that happened locally.

In our school, gym classes were required. Since I was too embarrassed to strip naked to take a shower in front of everyone, I failed gym. During high school I played basket ball, a guard because I couldn't make baskets and soon realized that I had no future in this sport. I tried softball, played in the outfield because I couldn't hit or catch a ball, so forget softball. But then, I tried field hockey and this was my sport. I played center halfback, loved to run and play hard, and our team was feared by all the teams we played. We played rough and refused to lose.

In the eighth grade, I decided that I would like to play in the band and maybe learn to play the flute or the clarinet. Carolyn and Peggy both played the clarinet in the band. One day, Carolyn asked me, "Hey Jeannie, why don't you come and play in the band. Maybe they need another clarinet."

"You know, Carolyn that sounds like a good idea. I'll go to the band room after school and ask Mr. Graves."

After school I approached Mr. Graves, the band director, and asked about joining the band. "Can you read music, Jeanne?"

"Yes, I took piano lessons."

"Well, I don't need a clarinet player but I do have a tenor saxophone that nobody is playing. Do you think that you'd be interested?"

"I can stop by for a lesson if you like, and try to play it."

"Great, stop by tomorrow after school and we will see if you like the saxophone. You know, we have no tenor saxophones in the whole school, so you'd be playing in both the junior and senior high bands."

Actually, that sounded like fun, so I replied, "That's ok with me. I'll see you tomorrow."

This was the beginning of my tenor sax lessons. The tenor sax is pretty big, something I hadn't counted on and I think one arm was bigger from carrying that huge case home to practice from the eighth to the twelfth grades. I enjoyed playing in both bands, the marching band, and made first chair in the state all star band my senior year. The Brown Company where my dad worked had a band also. I joined and played in the marching band and in the Sunday concerts in the park.

There was always a dance at school, a school concert given by the band, and recitals or plays at school given by the students. I had a walk on in a school play (my first and last), and even did a tap dance number in the talent show. Too embarrassing! I don't know how I dared to dance in front of all the kids at school.

Movies were 10 cents, so for a quarter, we went to the only movie theater, bought a candy bar and a drink. . The local community center was a great place to hang out, where we could swim, bowl with candlepins, play basketball, or hang out in the huge girl's room to gossip and smoke. Our group of girls were not part of the "popular" crowd, like the cheerleaders. We did our own thing. A favorite was our knitting group. We would meet at my house since my mom was a great knitter. She loved to have us there and said that we didn't get too much knitting done but we sure did a lot of talking and eating.

When I was in the tenth grade, we got a dial phone. Before that, we had a party line and our phone number was 1805-M and my friend Carolyn's number was 831-J. It was hard to make a call because someone was always using the phone on our party line and it was impolite to listen in or click on the line. The new dial phone was great but we could only call locally because calling long distance was expensive. If we were away from home, we had to use a phone in a telephone booth. Most of them were at gas stations and it cost 10 cents to make a call. Many times, the phone booth telephone book on a long chain would be really torn up and pages missing.

Our family didn't spend much time watching TV. We got out first black and white TV when I was in the fifth grade. It had rabbit ears that had to be turned to get a channel without snow on the screen. We only got about three channels. My dad liked to watch baseball games on Sunday afternoon. Ralph and I liked Howdy Doody and Clarabelle the cow. After school we watched the Mickey Mouse Club and Annette Funichello was my favorite mouseketeer. Bandstand was where I learned the new dances and heard new songs. There were favorite dancers I watched every week.

The junior prom was approaching and I had a date. Some of the girls and I had been riding to North Conway, a nearby town, to meet boys. My dad let me use his old Dodge with cardboard covering the holes in the back floor. (I was supposed to drive only locally). Our new boyfriends had a car and asked us if they could take us to the prom.

The afternoon of the prom as I was at the hairdresser's, I noticed red spots popping out on my arms as I was sitting under the dryer. When I returned home, the spots were all over my body.

"Mom, look at all my spots. Do you think that I have the measles?"

"It sure looks like the measles. You know that they are contagious, so you'd better stay home tonight."

"No way! I'm not staying home tonight." My mom had talked my dad into buying me my first strapless gown. It was baby blue with ruffles all over. "Powder me up and I'm going." I guess she knew it was useless to argue with me.

When Gerry, my date, came to the door with my corsage, I told him I had the measles, and he turned and walked down the stairs. He soon turned, laughing, and said, "I don't care!" Off we went, a whole group, to the junior prom, a party afterwards, and miraculously nobody got the measles. We had a ball dancing at the prom, and afterwards, as usual in our part of the country, piled into cars, went to the local drive in for junk food, and then to a classmate's camp in the woods for a party. On the way, Wendell, in the back seat underneath many others, yelled, "I have to puke!" The car pulled over and kids were running everywhere while Wendell puked, then all jumped back in. We all had a great time until the wee hours of the morning.

Senior year came so quickly that it was a blur. Classes seem to glide by. When I looked back, I never really studied much, just liked the challenge of testing and usually doing very well. I had at this time decided to go to nursing school and my mom had called to arrange an interview at a very good hospital about three hours away.

I was really nervous and didn't know what they did in an interview. My mom and I went in to the director's office together. The director stood up and shook our hands. Mrs. Stuart was so little, gray hair pulled back in a pug, and a big smile on her face. I felt like she was somebody's grandmother. She made us feel very comfortable and asked lots of questions.

"So, Jeanne, why do you think that you'd like to be a nurse?"

"Well, I have a lot of cousins and family friends that are nurses. I like to help people and I like science. Everyone respects nurses and they always will have a job. Your school has a good reputation and I would hope to be accepted here."

It was a long ride home and a long two weeks before the letter arrived that I had been accepted to the school of my choice. September would come very quickly and there were lots of things to do like work hard and save some money during the summer.

It was the end of the senior year and the senior prom was coming up.

"Jeannie, has anyone asked you to the prom?" Jeanne Ann was my closest friend, and she had a steady boyfriend named Jim and had a date, but I did not have a date yet.

"No, I don't have a date yet. I hope that somebody asks me to go."

"Jim has a good friend named Paul, and he would like to take you and we could double date."

"Let's go out some night before the dance so I can meet him and see if I like him. Is that ok?"

As it turned out, Paul was a great guy, we hit it off, and so it was a date. Senior prom, here I come.

"At least I didn't get measles this time," I told my mom.

"You look beautiful in your gown." my mom said. My dad and brother agreed and of course, pictures were taken on the front lawn. Jeanne Ann, Jim and Paul arrived, all dressed up, ready for a fun evening. Corsages on our wrists, guys in their tuxes, off we went in Jim's car to the senior prom. The dance was very nice and afterwards we all changed into hang out clothes, went to Sinibaldi's on the east side for pizzas, and out to a local party. We all had a great time. It was certainly not as exciting my junior prom, but a memorable prom night.

That last summer flew by, and soon I was packing. It was exciting and scary to leave home for the first time and be starting four years of nursing school. But, that's another story.

—

RALPH EMMETT PATRICK SHEVLIN
6/10/1947 -

Do I tell all or not? Well, some secrets from childhood have to remain untold. As adults, one day we started to tell my mother all the things we did that she never knew about. (She was too old to punish us then.) After about 30 minutes of unloading and Ralph and I having a great time shocking her, she finally said, "That's enough. I don't want to know any more."

As a child, he looked like an angel with his cute little round face, ice blue eyes like his mother, and curly blond hair. Teasing him when we were children was easy. I would, in French, call him a cute little blond baby, which would always set off a chase scene, ending with one of us getting hurt or punished. I would tease him, he would chase me, I would hit him, he would cry and I would get punished. Yup. That's how I remember it and don't believe Ralph if he tells you otherwise.

Ralph is as quiet as I am not. Two opposites. He hardly ever got in trouble, except for the time a policeman brought him to the front door for stealing apples from a neighbor's tree. I don't think that record is still on the books. He was a perfect student in school, all the way through high school. Not active in sports, he became the audio visual guru for all the school functions. To this day, he can build anything or fix anything. He even single handedly built a log cabin which, when finished, could have graced the cover of House Beautiful. But, don't ask him to throw anything out. In that respect, he is like his father. ("You might need it someday!")

If you want to go hiking or on an adventure, he's your man. He has been active in Boy Scouts, and always the big kid. Where you find all the kids congregating, you'll find him.

He retired from the phone company where he worked as a

lineman from his teens, and had a second career in maintenance at the local hospital. His daughter, Amy, is a registered nurse and daughter, Susan, is a pharmacist. He has four grandchildren and two adopted sons, Tyler and Stephen.

As children we were like gasoline and a match. Now he is my best friend, and if I ever need anything, I know he'll be there.

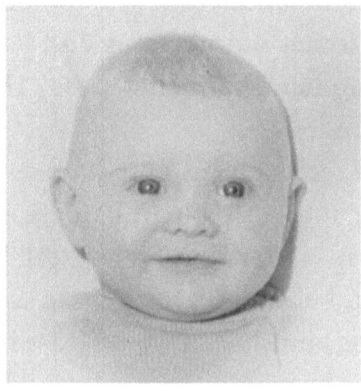
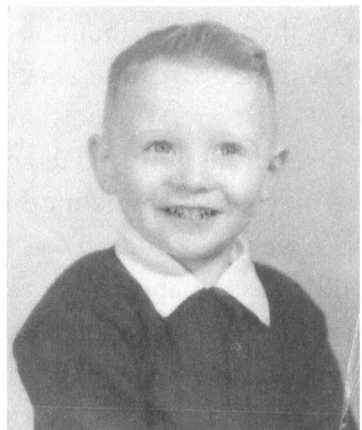

Ralph

Joan Roy, Perry Roy, Ralph and Jeanne

Ralph and Jeanne

Ralph and Jeanne

Ralph

FAMILY REUNIONS

1983

1990's

1995

1995

2000

Ralph and Jeanne

Tootsie, Dellie Dwyer, Jeanne and Ralph

FAMILY GENEOLOGY

TOUSSAINT/ROY
LOUIS ROY married PERPETUA____
AIME TOUSSAINT married DOMITILE GAMELIN
DOMITILE GAMELIN married _____
    Emne Gamelin married Helen Hildreth
      Nellie and Edward Hildreth
ALEXANDER ROY married CELINA TOUSSAINT
    George Roy married Delia Landry
    Bertha Roy married George John
    Henry Roy married Charlotte Perkins
    Alfred Roy married Hazel Henry
    Alice Roy married John Berard
    Emile Roy married Helen Hildreth
GEORGE AND DELIA'S CHILDREN
    Amey Joseph Roy (7/8/05 – 9/20/05)
    Eva Roy (8/1/12 – 8/20/12)
    Yvonne Roy (8/1/1912 – 11/11/08) Twin to Eva
    Gertrude Roy (1/20/09 -) married Kenneth Williams (1915 – 1996)
      Carol married Fred Doss
      Robert
    Henry (Pete) Roy(3/14/11 – 6/1/62) married Bertha Devoe
    Cleo Roy (2/18/15 – 8/14/85) married Dorothy Pilotte
      Phillip (12/20/35) married Norma ____
      Gary married Sylvia Chinard
        Debbie, Denise, Michelle, Craig, Mark
      Reginald (6/9/40) married Patty Champagne (1974)
        Nicole (1/16/60) and Becky (1961)
      Reginald married Marjorie McDonald
        Melinda (1/16/81) and Jason (12/19/85)

Joan (12/31/42 -) married Peter Bent
Perry (9/29/59) married Sharon Oakes
    Tiffany (6/26/75) - one child Hannah Ponse (1997)
    Benjamin (3/8/77)
    Katrina (9/1/70) married David Hall
        Jacob (12/17/91), Sophia (7/22/96), Samuel (10/12/98)
    Keith married Sara Ann Peters
        Alysmarie (3/3/95), Brett (4/24/98)
    Sara married Wayne Comtois
Perry married Carol Boucher
    Danny and Kristen
Dennis (3/4/57) married Diane Maurais
    Scott
Cleo Roy (2/18/15 – 8/14/85) married Theresa Maurais
    (her daughter married Cleo's son Dennis)
Amelia Roy (4/3/07 – 4/8/99) married Joseph O'Brien (2/2/37)
    Jack (4/3/29 -) married Geraldine Harney (8/29/33)
        Ann Marie (7/26/64)
        Andrew and Justin Avery (12/19/96)
        Kathleen (1/1/66) married Thomas Erdman
            Jared (2/12/92)
        Mary Bridget (5/22/77) married William Owens
            William (10/30/91), Jacob (6/10/93), Timothy (3/1/95)
        Maureen (4/30/61)
        Theresa (1/16/71) married Stephen Prosise (9/22/67)
    Richard (Dick) 1/4/32 -) married Barbara Ferris
    Mary Letitia (5/3/33 -) married Milton Rollo
        David (12/1/61) married _____
        Kathleen (10/10/65) married David Moores
            David, Jr. (7/24/91) and Megan (4/9/94)
        Kathleen married Ken Kadea Jr.
            Kailie (6/9/97)
    Phyllis (1/15/35) married Lawrence Stinehour (7/7/29)

    Patricia Jean (1/14/56) married Stephen Wightman
        Patricia Meryl (3/1/84)
            Patricia Meryl married Cody Jones
                Roosevelt
    Patrick (Rick) (2/8/60) married Michelle Knapp
        Sarah (11/18/93) and Sean (1/6/96)
    Patrick married _____
    William (Bill) (6/14/58) married Donna Brown
        Maxwell (8/18/83), Hallie (4/5/85), Kathleen (10/17/87),
        Rosa Lee (7/6/94)
            Maxwell married Lauren ___
                Linnea
            Kathleen married Richard Thomaine
                Rowan
        Craig (9/12/61) married Diana ___
        Beatrice Amelia
Phyllis Roy (7/24/17 – 7/5/06) married Emmett Shevlin
                (4/16/17 – 12/10/81)
    Jeanne Patricia (12/22/42) married Edward Blake
        Kimberly Ora (12/05/63) married David O'Brien (6/4/1962)
            Ashley Ora (2/19/91), Kyle (11/18/99)
        Mark Edward (7/10/65) married Jennifer_____
            Teresa (3/8/84) married Norman Martin III (3/9/79)
            Teresa is daughter of Mark Blake
                Alexis (2/24/04), Norman IV (3/10/07)
    Jeanne married Donald Hardwicke
    Jeanne married David Gates
        Julie Gates married Peter Kratimenos
        Julie Gates is daughter of David Gates
            Alexander
        Justin Gates
Ralph Emmett (6/10/47) married Betty McAllister
    Amy Jeanne (10/27/68) married Duane Kahkonen

Kenzie (12/24/99), Kori (6/22/02)
Susan Eileen (6/27/70) married Joseph Klementovich
Alex (8/17/00), Benjamin (7/4/02)
Ralph married Suzanne Rogers
Tyler (11/20/98), Stephen (10/2/03)
Ralph married Maryneth Mendiola
Hanna (3/19/94) (daughter of Maryneth)
Emile Roy (10/9/1897 - 10/12/64) married Helen Hildreth
(1901 – 1995)
Waldo married Dorothy ____
Robert, Patricia, Christine
Dorothy married Theodore Adamski
Geraldine (11/20/23 -) married Nathan McClure
Nathan Jr. married Rondi___(second marriage)
Nathan and Jacob
Mary Ann married Bob O'Dell
Patty Jean married Phillip Chris
Dennis married ____
Jason and Peter
Carol

THE FAMILY OF DELIA LANDRY ROY

Guillaume Mathurin Landry (2/3/1623 – 1/8/1689) married
 Gabrielle Barre (1628 – 7/4/1688)
Magliore Landry (?father of Joseph Landry)
Joseph Landry married Josephine Halle
Henry Landry (7/9/1890 -) Joseph's half brother
Delia Landry (12/14/1985 – 4/9/51) married George Roy
Joseph (Pete) Landry (3/17/88 – 2/3/52) married
Bernadette Langlais (1/26/90 – (8/30/81)
Pauline (9/5/26) married____

    Jeannette (3/4/13) married ___Gagnon
    Jean Paul (1/15/31) married____
    Therese (10/15/21) married Michael Trembley
    Leo (12/19/19) married_____
    Simone (5/5/14) married____
    Robert (3/25/16) married____
    Madeline (6/5/18) married ___
    Roger (7/5/23) married____

THE FAMILY OF EMMETT PATRICK SHEVLIN

Robert Shevlin (1806) relative from Queenstown, Cork County, Ireland

Willliam Murphy (1841) married Mary Alice Condon
  (Emmett Shevlin's great grandfather)

Cornelius Edward Murphy (1874) father of Patrick Murphy

Robert Murphy married Mary Cullen
    Mildred (1907 -1974) married Albert Wheeler (1911 – 1984)
        Albert
        Monica (1933 – 1968)
        Morris married Bea Tanguay
            Jay, Jill, Jayne and Joel
        Donny married Gert Lheureux
        Joan married ___Lamarre
            Brian, Bess, Bonnie and Brad
    Michael married Faith Hickey
    Robert married Dorothy Tourangeau
        Colleen married William Phinney
            Glen, Duane, John, and Maria
        Cullen married Mary Murphy (2015)
            Eileen married Chris Schmeke

  Jareth and Ben
 Colleen married David Harper
  Sean
 Colleen married ___
  Matthew
 Maureen
Raymond married Dorothy McDonald
 Lynn married Gary Pinette
  Kim
Henry married ___
 Frances married ____
 Howard (Ducky) married ____
  Linda, Mary, Michael and Bobby
Mary (1896 – 1931) married Patrick Shevlin
 Ralph (1919 – 1931) died at age sixteen
 Emmett Shevlin (4/16/17 – 12/10/81) married Phyllis Roy
  Jeanne and Ralph
 Joyce (1917 – 4/30/00) married John Noyes
  Shanna married ____ Harrison
 Robert married Doris____
  Doris Joyce and Robert Jr.
 Warren John married Pauline Strout
  Michael married Monique Adjami

EXTENDED FAMILY MEMBERS

Joseph O'Brien (Amelia Roy's husband) parents:
  James and Louise Hogan
John Francis O'Brien (4/6/21 – 4/1/94) brother of Joseph,
 married Dorothy Haskell (10/31/26) and
  Mary Agnes (5/16/55), James (9/10/57), Peter (2/3/59), Thomas
  Michael (10/5/62), Brigid (9/27/66)

Geraldine Harney, wife of Jack O'Brien:
    Parents, William Harney and Edity Predon

Lawrence Stinehour(husband of Phyllis O"Brien Stinehour)
    Parents: Eilliam and Emily Orgee

Edward Blake (husband of Jeanne Shevlin)
    Parents: George and Elnora
    Edward's siblings:
        Nancy married ____Willard
            Christopher and Jonathan
        Douglas

www.ingramcontent.com/pod-product-compliance
Lightning Source LLC
Chambersburg PA
CBHW021155080526
44588CB00008B/349